Table Of Contents

Chapter 1: Introduction to Programming Languages

What are Programming Languages?

Programming languages are essential tools for anyone looking to enter the world of technology. They are sets of instructions that allow computers to perform specific tasks, such as running applications, processing data, and controlling hardware. Programming languages are the foundation of software development, enabling developers to create everything from websites and mobile apps to artificial intelligence algorithms and cybersecurity solutions.

In the realm of web development skills, programming languages like HTML, CSS, and JavaScript are commonly used to create dynamic and interactive websites. These languages allow developers to design user-friendly interfaces, add animations and effects, and optimize websites for search engines. Understanding programming languages is crucial for web developers to build responsive and visually appealing websites that meet the needs of their clients and users.

For those interested in mobile app development skills, programming languages such as Java, Swift, and Kotlin are popular choices for creating mobile applications for iOS and Android devices. These languages enable developers to design intuitive user interfaces, integrate with device features like GPS and camera, and provide seamless user experiences. By mastering programming languages, mobile app developers can create innovative and user-friendly apps that cater to the preferences and needs of mobile users.

In the field of cybersecurity skills, programming languages play a critical role in developing secure software, identifying vulnerabilities, and implementing protective measures. Languages like Python, C++, and Ruby are used to write scripts, automate security tasks, and analyze data for potential threats. Understanding programming languages is essential for cybersecurity professionals to detect and respond to cyber attacks, protect sensitive information, and safeguard digital assets.

Whether you are interested in programming language skills, user experience design skills, artificial intelligence skills, or any other tech-related field, mastering programming languages is a valuable asset. By learning the fundamentals of programming languages like Python, Java, and C++, you can enhance your problem-solving abilities, improve your critical thinking skills, and advance your career in the rapidly evolving tech industry. Programming languages are the building blocks of technology, empowering individuals to create innovative solutions, drive digital transformation, and shape the future of the digital world.

Importance of Learning Multiple Programming Languages

In today's fast-paced and ever-evolving digital landscape, learning multiple programming languages has become increasingly important for individuals looking to expand their tech skills. Whether you are interested in web development, mobile app development, cybersecurity, programming language skills, user experience design, or artificial intelligence, mastering more than one programming language can open up a world of opportunities for you. This subchapter will delve into the significance of learning multiple programming languages and how it can benefit individuals in various tech-related niches.

One of the key reasons why learning multiple programming languages is crucial is that it allows individuals to adapt to different projects and technologies. Each programming language has its own strengths and weaknesses, and by being proficient in more than one language, you can choose the most suitable language for a particular project. For example, Python is often used in data science and artificial intelligence, while Java is commonly used in mobile app development. By having a diverse skill set, you can tackle a wider range of projects and excel in different areas of tech.

Furthermore, learning multiple programming languages can enhance your problem-solving skills and creativity. Each language has its own unique syntax and features, and by understanding different programming paradigms, you can approach problems from multiple perspectives. This can help you think outside the box and come up with innovative solutions to complex tech challenges. Additionally, mastering multiple languages can boost your confidence and self-efficacy, as you gain a deeper understanding of various programming concepts and techniques.

In the competitive tech industry, having expertise in multiple programming languages can give you a competitive edge and increase your marketability. Employers are often looking for candidates who can demonstrate versatility and adaptability, and being proficient in multiple languages shows that you are a well-rounded and resourceful tech professional. Whether you are a web developer, mobile app developer, cybersecurity expert, or AI specialist, having a diverse skill set can set you apart from other candidates and open up more job opportunities for you.

In conclusion, learning multiple programming languages is essential for individuals looking to enhance their tech skills and excel in various niches such as web development, mobile app development, cybersecurity, programming language skills, user experience design, and artificial intelligence. By mastering more than one language, you can adapt to different projects, improve your problem-solving abilities, boost your creativity, and increase your marketability in the tech industry. So, whether you are just starting out in your tech career or looking to advance to the next level, make sure to invest time and effort in learning multiple programming languages to stay ahead of the curve and achieve your professional goals.

Overview of Python, Java, and C++

In the world of technology, programming languages play a crucial role in developing various applications and software. Three popular programming languages that are widely used in the industry are Python, Java, and C++. Each of these languages has its own unique features and capabilities that make them suitable for different types of projects. In this subchapter, we will provide an overview of Python, Java, and C++ to help you understand their strengths and weaknesses.

Python is a high-level programming language known for its simplicity and readability. It is widely used in web development, data analysis, artificial intelligence, and machine learning. Python's syntax is easy to learn and understand, making it a popular choice for beginners. With a large standard library and a vibrant community of developers, Python is a versatile language that can be used for a wide range of projects.

Java is a robust and versatile programming language that is commonly used for developing enterprise-level applications, mobile apps, and web applications. Java's platform independence allows developers to write code once and run it on any device that supports Java. With its strong typing system and object-oriented programming features, Java is suitable for building large and complex software systems. Java is also known for its security features, making it a popular choice for cybersecurity professionals.

C++ is a powerful and efficient programming language that is commonly used for system programming, game development, and high-performance applications. C++ allows developers to have more control over the hardware and memory management, making it a preferred choice for building applications that require high performance. With its support for object-oriented programming and low-level programming, C++ is a versatile language that can be used for a wide range of projects.

In conclusion, Python, Java, and C++ are three popular programming languages that are widely used in the industry for various purposes. Python is known for its simplicity and versatility, Java is renowned for its platform independence and security features, and C++ is valued for its power and efficiency. Whether you are learning new tech skills for web development, mobile app development, cybersecurity, programming language skills, user experience design, or artificial intelligence, mastering these languages will help you become a proficient developer in your chosen niche.

Chapter 2: Python Basics

Introduction to Python

Python is a powerful and versatile programming language that has become increasingly popular in recent years. In this subchapter, we will provide an introduction to Python for those who are new to programming or looking to expand their skills in the tech industry. Whether you are interested in web development, mobile app development, cybersecurity, programming languages, user experience design, or artificial intelligence, Python is a valuable language to learn.

Python is known for its simplicity and readability, making it an ideal language for beginners. Its syntax is clear and concise, making it easy to understand and write code. Python also has a large standard library that provides a wide range of modules and packages for various tasks, such as web development, data analysis, and machine learning. This makes Python a versatile language that can be used for a wide range of applications.

One of the key features of Python is its versatility. It can be used for a wide range of tasks, from simple scripting to complex web applications. Python is also cross-platform, meaning that it can run on different operating systems, such as Windows, macOS, and Linux. This makes it a flexible language that can be used in a variety of contexts.

Python is also a popular language in the tech industry, with many companies using it for web development, data analysis, and machine learning. By learning Python, you can increase your job prospects and open up new opportunities in the tech industry. Whether you are interested in developing websites, mobile apps, or cybersecurity tools, Python can help you achieve your goals.

In this subchapter, we will cover the basics of Python, including data types, variables, control structures, functions, and modules. We will also provide examples and exercises to help you practice your skills and reinforce your understanding of the material. By the end of this subchapter, you will have a solid foundation in Python and be ready to tackle more advanced topics in the language.

Data Types and Variables in Python

In the world of programming, understanding data types and variables is crucial for creating efficient and effective code. In Python, a popular programming language known for its simplicity and readability, data types and variables play a key role in defining and manipulating data. This subchapter will delve into the fundamentals of data types and variables in Python, providing a solid foundation for those looking to master this versatile language.

Python offers several built-in data types, including integers, floats, strings, lists, tuples, and dictionaries. Each data type serves a specific purpose and allows programmers to store and manipulate different kinds of data. For example, integers are used to represent whole numbers, floats are used for decimal numbers, and strings are used for text. Understanding how to work with these data types is essential for effectively writing Python code.

Variables in Python serve as placeholders for storing data values. When a variable is assigned a value, it is stored in the computer's memory and can be accessed and manipulated throughout the program. Variables are dynamically typed in Python, meaning that you do not need to explicitly declare the data type of a variable before using it. This flexibility makes Python a popular choice for beginners and experienced programmers alike.

When working with variables in Python, it is important to follow naming conventions to ensure clarity and readability in your code. Variable names should be descriptive and meaningful, reflecting the purpose of the data they store. Avoid using reserved keywords or special characters in variable names, as this can lead to errors and confusion when running your code. By following best practices for naming variables, you can make your code more understandable and maintainable.

Overall, mastering data types and variables in Python is essential for anyone looking to excel in web development, mobile app development, cybersecurity, programming language skills, user experience design, or artificial intelligence. By understanding how data types work and how variables are used, you can write clean, efficient code that performs optimally. This subchapter will provide you with the knowledge and skills needed to confidently work with data types and variables in Python, setting you on the path to programming language mastery.

Control Flow in Python

Control flow in Python is an essential concept that every programmer must understand in order to effectively write code. In Python, control flow refers to the order in which statements are executed in a program. By using control flow structures such as loops and conditional statements, programmers can dictate how their code should behave under different circumstances.

One of the most common control flow structures in Python is the "if-else" statement. This statement allows programmers to execute different blocks of code based on whether a certain condition is true or false. For example, if a user enters the correct password, the program may grant them access to a secure system. If the password is incorrect, the program may display an error message.

Another important control flow structure in Python is the "for loop." This loop allows programmers to iterate over a sequence of items, such as a list or a string, and perform a certain action on each item. For example, a programmer may use a for loop to calculate the total sum of a list of numbers or to print out each character in a string.

In addition to the "if-else" statement and the "for loop," Python also supports other control flow structures such as the "while loop" and the "break" and "continue" statements. The "while loop" allows programmers to repeatedly execute a block of code as long as a certain condition is true. The "break" statement allows programmers to exit a loop prematurely, while the "continue" statement allows programmers to skip the rest of the current iteration and move on to the next one.

Overall, mastering control flow in Python is crucial for anyone looking to become proficient in programming. By understanding how to use control flow structures effectively, programmers can create more efficient and organized code that meets the needs of their users. Whether you are learning new tech skills for web development, mobile app development, cybersecurity, programming languages, user experience design, or artificial intelligence, a solid understanding of control flow in Python will serve you well in your career.

Chapter 3: Java Fundamentals

Introduction to Java

In the world of technology, Java is a powerful and versatile programming language that is widely used in various industries. Whether you are interested in web development, mobile app development, cybersecurity, programming language skills, user experience design, or artificial intelligence, Java is a language that can help you achieve your goals. In this subchapter, we will introduce you to the basics of Java and help you understand its key concepts and features.

Java was developed by Sun Microsystems in the mid-1990s and has since become one of the most popular programming languages in the world. It is known for its portability, as Java programs can run on any device that has a Java Virtual Machine (JVM) installed. This makes Java an ideal choice for developing cross-platform applications that can be used on different operating systems.

One of the key features of Java is its object-oriented programming (OOP) paradigm. This means that Java programs are made up of objects that interact with each other to perform specific tasks. By using objects, developers can create modular and reusable code that is easier to maintain and debug. Understanding OOP principles is essential for mastering Java and becoming a proficient programmer.

Another important aspect of Java is its robust standard library, which provides a wide range of pre-built classes and methods for performing common tasks. This makes it easier for developers to write efficient and reliable code without having to reinvent the wheel. By leveraging the power of the Java standard library, you can save time and focus on building innovative solutions for your projects.

In conclusion, Java is a versatile and powerful programming language that can help you develop a wide range of applications for web development, mobile app development, cybersecurity, programming language skills, user experience design, and artificial intelligence. By mastering the fundamentals of Java, you can unlock endless possibilities and take your tech skills to the next level. Whether you are a beginner or an experienced developer, learning Java is a valuable investment in your career and will open up new opportunities in the ever-evolving tech industry.

Object-Oriented Programming in Java

Object-oriented programming is a crucial concept to understand when delving into the world of Java programming. In this subchapter, we will explore the fundamentals of object-oriented programming in Java and how it can be utilized to create powerful and efficient software applications. By mastering these principles, individuals learning new tech skills can enhance their abilities in various niches such as web development, mobile app development, cybersecurity, programming language skills, user experience design, and artificial intelligence.

At the core of object-oriented programming in Java is the concept of classes and objects. A class serves as a blueprint for creating objects, which are instances of that class. This allows programmers to encapsulate data and behavior within a single entity, making it easier to manage and manipulate. By understanding how to define classes and create objects in Java, individuals can organize their code in a more structured and logical manner.

Another key aspect of object-oriented programming in Java is inheritance. Inheritance allows classes to inherit attributes and methods from a parent class, enabling code reusability and promoting a hierarchical structure. By utilizing inheritance, individuals can reduce redundancy in their code and create more scalable and maintainable software applications. Understanding how to implement inheritance in Java is essential for developing efficient and well-structured programs.

Polymorphism is another important concept in object-oriented programming that individuals learning new tech skills should be familiar with. Polymorphism allows objects to be treated as instances of their parent class, enabling flexibility and extensibility in code. By leveraging polymorphism in Java, programmers can write more generic and flexible code that can adapt to different scenarios and requirements. Mastering polymorphism is crucial for individuals looking to enhance their programming language skills and develop more dynamic software applications.

Lastly, encapsulation is a fundamental principle of object-oriented programming that plays a vital role in Java development. Encapsulation involves bundling data and methods within a class and controlling access to them through access modifiers such as public, private, and protected. By encapsulating data and behavior, individuals can create more secure and robust software applications that are less prone to errors and vulnerabilities. Understanding how to apply encapsulation in Java is essential for individuals looking to enhance their cybersecurity skills and develop more secure software solutions.

Java Syntax and Data Structures

In this subchapter, we will delve into the fundamental concepts of Java syntax and data structures. Java is a powerful and versatile programming language that is widely used in various industries such as web development, mobile app development, cybersecurity, and artificial intelligence. Understanding the syntax of Java and how to effectively use data structures is essential for anyone looking to master this programming language.

Java syntax refers to the rules that govern how Java code is written and interpreted by the Java compiler. It includes rules for declaring variables, defining classes and methods, and implementing control flow structures such as loops and conditionals. By mastering Java syntax, you will be able to write clean, efficient, and error-free code that is easy to maintain and understand.

Data structures are essential for organizing and manipulating data in Java programs. They provide a way to store and retrieve data efficiently, allowing you to perform a wide range of operations such as searching, sorting, and filtering. Common data structures in Java include arrays, lists, stacks, queues, and maps. By understanding how these data structures work and when to use them, you can optimize the performance of your Java programs and build more robust and scalable applications.

When it comes to web development skills, knowing Java syntax and data structures is crucial for building dynamic and interactive websites. Java is often used in combination with technologies such as JavaServer Pages (JSP) and JavaServer Faces (JSF) to create web applications that can handle complex business logic and large amounts of data. By mastering Java syntax and data structures, you will be able to develop secure and responsive web applications that meet the needs of modern users.

In conclusion, mastering Java syntax and data structures is essential for anyone looking to excel in the fields of web development, mobile app development, cybersecurity, programming language skills, user experience design, and artificial intelligence. By understanding the fundamental concepts of Java syntax and data structures, you will be able to write efficient, reliable, and scalable code that meets the demands of today's technology-driven world. So, dive into this subchapter with an open mind and a thirst for knowledge, and you will be well on your way to becoming a Java programming master.

Chapter 4: C++ Essentials

Introduction to C++

Welcome to the world of programming with C++! In this subchapter, we will explore the fundamentals of the C++ programming language, its history, and how it is used in various fields such as web development, mobile app development, cybersecurity, programming language skills, user experience design, and artificial intelligence.

C++ is a powerful and versatile programming language that was first developed by Bjarne Stroustrup in the early 1980s. It is an extension of the C programming language, with added features such as object-oriented programming and generic programming. C++ is known for its efficiency, speed, and flexibility, making it a popular choice for building high-performance applications.

For those interested in web development, C++ can be used to create backend systems, server-side applications, and APIs. Its speed and efficiency make it a great choice for handling complex computations and heavy data processing tasks. In mobile app development, C++ is often used for building high-performance games, graphics-intensive applications, and system-level programming for mobile devices.

Cybersecurity professionals rely on C++ for developing secure and reliable software systems, encryption algorithms, and network protocols. Its low-level capabilities make it ideal for writing code that interacts directly with hardware, providing fine-grained control over system resources. In the field of artificial intelligence, C++ is used for developing machine learning algorithms, neural networks, and computer vision applications that require high-speed processing and optimization.

Whether you are a beginner learning new tech skills or a seasoned programmer looking to expand your knowledge, understanding C++ is essential for mastering the art of programming. In the following sections, we will delve deeper into the syntax, data types, control structures, and advanced features of C++, providing you with the tools you need to become a proficient C++ programmer. Get ready to unlock the full potential of C++ and take your programming skills to the next level!

Pointers and Memory Management in C++

Pointers and memory management in C++ are fundamental concepts that every programmer must understand in order to write efficient and error-free code. In C++, a pointer is a variable that stores the memory address of another variable. Pointers are powerful tools that allow programmers to manipulate memory directly, but they can also be a source of bugs if not used carefully. Understanding how to work with pointers is essential for anyone learning new tech skills, especially those in the fields of web development, mobile app development, cybersecurity, programming language, user experience design, and artificial intelligence.

Memory management in C++ is the process of allocating and deallocating memory during the execution of a program. In C++, memory management is done manually by the programmer using functions such as new and delete. This gives the programmer more control over memory allocation but also introduces the risk of memory leaks and other memory-related errors. Learning how to properly manage memory in C++ is crucial for anyone working in the tech industry, as inefficient memory management can lead to performance issues and security vulnerabilities in software.

One important concept to understand when working with pointers in C++ is pointer arithmetic. Pointer arithmetic allows programmers to perform arithmetic operations on pointers, such as adding or subtracting an offset to move to a different memory location. This can be useful when working with arrays or other data structures that are stored in contiguous memory locations. However, it is important to be careful when using pointer arithmetic, as it can easily lead to out-of-bounds memory access and other bugs if not done correctly.

Another important topic related to pointers and memory management in C++ is the concept of memory leaks. A memory leak occurs when a program allocates memory but fails to deallocate it when it is no longer needed. This can lead to a gradual loss of available memory, eventually causing the program to crash or slow down significantly. Learning how to identify and prevent memory leaks is essential for anyone working in the tech industry, as memory leaks can be a common source of bugs in software.

In conclusion, understanding pointers and memory management in C++ is essential for anyone learning new tech skills, especially those in the fields of web development, mobile app development, cybersecurity, programming language, user experience design, and artificial intelligence. By mastering these concepts, programmers can write more efficient and reliable code, leading to better performance and security in their software projects. It is important to practice working with pointers and memory management in C++ to become proficient in these fundamental concepts and avoid common pitfalls that can arise when working with memory in programming.

Advanced C++ Concepts

In the world of programming, mastering advanced concepts in C++ is essential for anyone looking to excel in the field of technology. In this subchapter, we will delve into some of the most advanced concepts in C++ that will take your programming skills to the next level. Whether you are a web developer, mobile app developer, cybersecurity expert, or aspiring AI engineer, understanding these concepts will set you apart from the competition and open up new opportunities in the tech industry.

One of the key advanced concepts in C++ is template metaprogramming, which allows for the creation of generic code that can be used with multiple data types. By leveraging templates, you can write code that is more flexible, reusable, and efficient. This is particularly useful in web development, where you may need to work with a variety of data types and structures.

Another important concept to master in C++ is object-oriented programming (OOP). OOP allows you to organize your code into classes and objects, making it easier to manage and maintain complex software projects. This is crucial for mobile app development, where you may be working on large-scale projects with multiple components and dependencies.

Understanding memory management in C++ is also crucial for anyone looking to excel in the tech industry. Memory leaks and inefficient memory allocation can lead to performance issues and security vulnerabilities in your code. By mastering concepts such as pointers, references, and dynamic memory allocation, you can write more efficient and secure code for your applications.

Lastly, mastering advanced C++ concepts such as multithreading and concurrency will make you a valuable asset in the field of artificial intelligence. As AI continues to revolutionize industries such as healthcare, finance, and transportation, the ability to write efficient and scalable code that can handle complex computations in parallel will be in high demand. By understanding these advanced concepts in C++, you will be well-equipped to tackle the challenges of AI development and contribute to cutting-edge technology projects.

In conclusion, mastering advanced concepts in C++ is essential for anyone looking to excel in the tech industry. Whether you are a web developer, mobile app developer, cybersecurity expert, or aspiring AI engineer, understanding these concepts will set you apart from the competition and open up new opportunities in the field of technology. By delving into topics such as template metaprogramming, object-oriented programming, memory management, and multithreading, you will be well-equipped to tackle the challenges of modern software development and make a meaningful impact in the tech industry.

Chapter 5: Web Development with Python, Java, and C++

Building Websites with Python

In this subchapter, we will explore the exciting world of building websites with Python. Python is a powerful and versatile programming language that is widely used in web development due to its simplicity and readability. Whether you are looking to create a personal blog, a business website, or a complex web application, Python has the tools and libraries to help you bring your ideas to life.

One of the key advantages of using Python for web development is its extensive collection of frameworks such as Django and Flask. These frameworks provide developers with pre-built tools and libraries that streamline the process of building websites, making it easier to create dynamic and interactive web applications. By learning how to use these frameworks, you can quickly create professional-looking websites without having to reinvent the wheel.

Another important aspect of building websites with Python is understanding how to work with databases. Python offers support for a wide range of database systems, including MySQL, PostgreSQL, and SQLite, allowing you to store and retrieve data from your website efficiently. By mastering database management in Python, you can create websites that are not only visually appealing but also highly functional and responsive to user input.

Additionally, Python's versatility extends beyond just building websites. With Python, you can also develop mobile applications, enhance cybersecurity measures, create advanced programming language tools, design user-friendly interfaces, and even delve into the exciting field of artificial intelligence. By honing your skills in Python web development, you open the door to a wide range of career opportunities in various tech sectors.

In conclusion, building websites with Python is a rewarding endeavor that can lead to a fulfilling career in web development, mobile app development, cybersecurity, programming languages, user experience design, or artificial intelligence. By mastering the tools and frameworks available in Python, you can create innovative and dynamic websites that engage users and provide valuable services. So, whether you are a beginner or an experienced developer looking to expand your skill set, learning how to build websites with Python is an essential step towards becoming a proficient and versatile tech professional.

Creating Web Applications with Java

Creating web applications with Java is an essential skill for individuals looking to enhance their web development skills. Java is a versatile programming language that is widely used in developing dynamic and interactive web applications. By mastering Java for web development, individuals can create powerful and efficient web applications that meet the needs of users while also adhering to industry standards and best practices.

One of the key advantages of using Java for web development is its compatibility with a wide range of platforms and devices. Java web applications can run on any device that supports Java, making them accessible to a broad audience. This versatility is especially important for individuals looking to expand their mobile app development skills, as Java can be used to create mobile applications that work seamlessly across different devices and operating systems.

In addition to its compatibility, Java offers a robust set of tools and libraries that make it easy to develop secure and scalable web applications. Individuals looking to enhance their cybersecurity skills will benefit from learning Java, as it provides built-in security features that help protect web applications from malicious attacks. By mastering Java for web development, individuals can create web applications that are not only user-friendly but also highly secure and reliable.

Furthermore, Java is an excellent programming language for individuals looking to improve their programming language skills. Java's syntax is easy to learn and understand, making it a great language for beginners to start with. By learning Java for web development, individuals can gain a solid foundation in programming principles that can be applied to other languages and technologies.

Overall, mastering Java for web development is essential for individuals looking to enhance their user experience design skills, artificial intelligence skills, and overall proficiency in programming. By learning Java, individuals can create innovative and engaging web applications that meet the demands of today's digital landscape. With its versatility, security features, and ease of use, Java is a valuable tool for anyone looking to excel in the world of web development.

Web Development Tools in C++

If you are looking to enhance your web development skills, mastering C++ can open up a world of possibilities. C++ is a powerful programming language that is commonly used in web development to create efficient and high-performing applications. By familiarizing yourself with the various web development tools available in C++, you can streamline your development process and create dynamic and interactive websites.

One of the most popular web development tools in C++ is the "CppCMS" framework. CppCMS is a high-performance web development framework that allows developers to build fast and scalable web applications. With CppCMS, you can easily create dynamic web pages, handle user input, and interact with databases. This framework is ideal for building complex web applications that require high levels of performance and security.

Another essential web development tool in C++ is the "Wt" library. Wt is a web GUI library that allows developers to create interactive

21

web applications using C++. With Wt, you can easily build web interfaces that are responsive and user-friendly. This library provides a rich set of widgets and controls that enable you to create sophisticated web applications with minimal effort. Whether you are developing a simple website or a complex web application, Wt can help you bring your ideas to life.

For those interested in mobile app development skills, C++ offers a range of tools and frameworks that can help you create powerful and feature-rich mobile applications. By mastering C++ and its associated web development tools, you can build cross-platform mobile apps that run seamlessly on both Android and iOS devices. With C++, you can leverage the power of native app development to create fast and efficient mobile applications that provide a seamless user experience.

In conclusion, mastering C++ and its web development tools can help you enhance your programming language skills and open up new opportunities in web development, mobile app development, cybersecurity, user experience design, and artificial intelligence. By familiarizing yourself with the various web development tools available in C++, you can become a more versatile and skilled developer, capable of creating innovative and cutting-edge applications. So, whether you are a beginner or an experienced programmer looking to expand your skill set, learning C++ and its web development tools can help you achieve your goals in the tech industry.

Chapter 6: Mobile App Development with Python, Java, and C++

Developing Mobile Apps with Python

In this subchapter, we will delve into the exciting world of developing mobile apps with Python. Python is a versatile programming language that is well-suited for mobile app development due to its simplicity and readability. By mastering Python, you will be equipped with the skills necessary to create powerful and innovative mobile applications that can run on a variety of devices.

One of the key advantages of using Python for mobile app development is its extensive library of tools and frameworks. Python offers a wide range of libraries such as Kivy, Pygame, and BeeWare that make it easy to build mobile apps with rich features and functionalities. These libraries provide developers with the resources they need to create visually appealing and user-friendly mobile applications that deliver a seamless user experience.

When developing mobile apps with Python, it is important to consider the unique challenges and requirements of mobile platforms. Mobile devices have limited resources compared to desktop computers, so it is crucial to optimize your code for performance and efficiency. By following best practices and utilizing Python's built-in tools for optimization, you can ensure that your mobile app runs smoothly and efficiently on any device.

Furthermore, Python's cross-platform compatibility makes it an ideal choice for mobile app development. With Python, you can write code once and deploy it on multiple platforms, saving time and effort in the development process. Whether you are targeting iOS, Android, or Windows devices, Python allows you to reach a wider audience with your mobile app and maximize its potential for success.

In conclusion, developing mobile apps with Python is a rewarding and exciting endeavor that can open up a world of opportunities in the tech industry. By honing your Python skills and mastering the art of mobile app development, you will be well-equipped to create innovative and impactful mobile applications that cater to the needs of modern users. So, roll up your sleeves and get ready to embark on a journey of creativity and discovery as you dive into the world of mobile app development with Python.

Android App Development with Java

In this subchapter, we will delve into the exciting world of Android app development with Java. Java is a widely used programming language for creating mobile applications, and learning how to develop Android apps with Java can open up many opportunities for those looking to expand their tech skills. Whether you are interested in web development, mobile app development, cybersecurity, programming language mastery, user experience design, or artificial intelligence, learning Android app development with Java is a valuable skill to have in your toolkit.

When it comes to web development skills, understanding how to create Android apps with Java can give you a competitive edge in the job market. Many companies are looking for developers who can create mobile applications that are user-friendly and visually appealing. By mastering Android app development with Java, you can enhance your web development skills and create dynamic and interactive mobile applications that will impress potential employers.

For those interested in mobile app development skills, learning Java for Android app development is essential. Java is a versatile programming language that is used by millions of developers worldwide to create mobile applications for Android devices. By mastering Java for Android app development, you can create high-quality apps that run smoothly on a variety of devices and screen sizes.

Cybersecurity skills are in high demand, and understanding how to develop secure Android apps with Java is a valuable skill to have in today's digital landscape. By learning best practices for secure coding and implementing security measures in your Android applications, you can help protect user data and prevent cyber attacks. Mastering Android app development with Java can give you the skills you need to create secure and reliable mobile applications.

In conclusion, learning Android app development with Java is a valuable skill for anyone looking to enhance their tech skills in web development, mobile app development, cybersecurity, programming language mastery, user experience design, or artificial intelligence. By mastering Java for Android app development, you can create innovative and user-friendly mobile applications that will help you stand out in the competitive tech industry. So, whether you are a beginner or an experienced developer, dive into the world of Android app development with Java and unlock endless possibilities for your tech career.

iOS App Development with C++

In today's digital age, mobile app development has become an essential skill for anyone looking to stay competitive in the tech industry. With the rise of iOS devices such as iPhones and iPads, learning how to develop apps for the iOS platform has never been more important. In this subchapter, we will explore how you can leverage your knowledge of C++ to develop iOS apps, opening up a world of possibilities for your career in tech.

iOS app development with C++ offers a unique advantage for developers who are already familiar with the C++ programming language. By using C++ in conjunction with tools like Objective-C or Swift, developers can create powerful and efficient iOS apps that take full advantage of the platform's capabilities. This combination of languages allows for seamless integration with existing C++ codebases, making it easier to port applications to iOS and reach a wider audience.

One of the key benefits of using C++ for iOS app development is its performance. C++ is a high-performance language that allows developers to create apps that run smoothly and efficiently on iOS devices. This is particularly important for mobile app development, where performance can make or break the user experience. By leveraging the power of C++, developers can create apps that are fast, responsive, and optimized for the iOS platform.

Another advantage of using C++ for iOS app development is its versatility. C++ is a flexible language that can be used to create a wide range of apps, from simple utility apps to complex, feature-rich applications. Whether you're developing a game, a productivity tool, or a social networking app, C++ provides the tools and capabilities you need to bring your vision to life on the iOS platform.

In conclusion, iOS app development with C++ is a valuable skill for anyone looking to expand their tech skills and reach new audiences through mobile app development. By leveraging the power and versatility of C++, developers can create high-performance, feature-rich apps that run seamlessly on iOS devices. Whether you're a web developer, cybersecurity expert, or aspiring AI specialist, mastering iOS app development with C++ can open up a world of opportunities in the tech industry.

Chapter 7: Introduction to Cybersecurity

Understanding Cybersecurity Threats

In the fast-paced world of technology, understanding cybersecurity threats is essential for anyone learning new tech skills. Whether you are delving into web development, mobile app development, cybersecurity, programming languages, user experience design, or artificial intelligence, being aware of potential threats can help you protect your work and data. In this subchapter, we will explore the various cybersecurity threats that exist in today's digital landscape and how you can safeguard your projects against them.

One of the most common cybersecurity threats is malware, which includes viruses, worms, and Trojan horses. These malicious software programs can infect your computer or network, causing damage to your files and stealing sensitive information. By learning how to recognize and prevent malware attacks, you can protect your projects and data from being compromised.

Another prevalent cybersecurity threat is phishing, where attackers use deceptive emails or websites to trick users into revealing their personal information, such as passwords or credit card details. By educating yourself on how to identify phishing attempts and practicing good security habits, you can reduce the risk of falling victim to these scams and protect your valuable data.

Additionally, ransomware is a growing cybersecurity threat that encrypts your files and demands payment for their release. By implementing strong security measures, such as regularly backing up your data and keeping your software up to date, you can mitigate the risk of falling prey to ransomware attacks and ensure that your projects remain secure.

Overall, understanding cybersecurity threats is crucial for anyone learning new tech skills, as it allows you to protect your work and data from potential harm. By staying informed about the latest threats and implementing best practices for cybersecurity, you can safeguard your projects and focus on honing your skills in web development, mobile app development, cybersecurity, programming languages, user experience design, or artificial intelligence.

Secure Coding Practices

Secure coding practices are essential for anyone learning new tech skills, especially in fields such as web development, mobile app development, cybersecurity, programming languages, user experience design, and artificial intelligence. By following secure coding practices, individuals can protect their systems and applications from potential vulnerabilities and cyber attacks. In this subchapter, we will explore some of the key principles and techniques for secure coding.

One of the fundamental principles of secure coding is input validation. It is crucial to validate all user input to prevent malicious code from being executed on a system. By validating input, developers can ensure that only safe and expected data is processed by their applications. Failure to validate input can lead to security vulnerabilities such as SQL injection, cross-site scripting, and buffer overflows.

Another important aspect of secure coding is proper handling of errors and exceptions. Error handling is essential for identifying and resolving issues that may arise during the execution of an application. By implementing robust error handling mechanisms, developers can prevent sensitive information from being exposed to potential attackers. Additionally, error handling can help improve the overall stability and reliability of an application.

Secure coding also involves implementing secure authentication and authorization mechanisms. Authentication verifies the identity of users accessing an application, while authorization determines the actions that each user is allowed to perform. By using strong authentication methods such as multi-factor authentication and implementing role-based access control, developers can enhance the security of their applications and protect sensitive data from unauthorized access.

Encryption is another key aspect of secure coding practices. By encrypting sensitive data in transit and at rest, developers can prevent unauthorized access to confidential information. Using strong encryption algorithms and secure protocols can help protect data from potential eavesdropping and interception. Additionally, developers should ensure that encryption keys are securely stored and managed to prevent unauthorized access.

In conclusion, secure coding practices are essential for individuals learning new tech skills in various niches such as web development, mobile app development, cybersecurity, programming languages, user experience design, and artificial intelligence. By following principles such as input validation, error handling, authentication, authorization, and encryption, developers can enhance the security of their applications and protect them from potential vulnerabilities and cyber attacks. By incorporating secure coding practices into their development workflow, individuals can build secure and robust applications that meet the highest standards of security and privacy.

Cybersecurity Tools and Techniques

In today's digital age, cybersecurity has become more important than ever. As technology continues to advance, so do the threats and risks associated with it. It is crucial for individuals learning new tech skills, such as web development, mobile app development, programming languages, user experience design, artificial intelligence, and cybersecurity, to have a solid understanding of cybersecurity tools and techniques to protect their work and data.

One of the most important cybersecurity tools is a firewall, which acts as a barrier between a trusted network and an untrusted network. Firewalls help prevent unauthorized access to your system and can be configured to block specific types of traffic. It is essential for individuals in the tech industry to familiarize themselves with firewalls and how to properly configure them to protect their networks and data.

Another essential cybersecurity tool is antivirus software, which helps detect and remove malicious software from your computer. Antivirus software scans your system for any suspicious files or programs and alerts you if it finds any threats. It is crucial for individuals in the tech industry to regularly update their antivirus software to ensure they are protected against the latest threats.

Encryption is another important cybersecurity technique that individuals learning new tech skills should be familiar with. Encryption involves encoding data in such a way that only authorized parties can access it. By encrypting sensitive information, individuals can protect their data from unauthorized access and ensure its confidentiality.

In addition to these tools and techniques, individuals in the tech industry should also be aware of best practices for cybersecurity, such as regularly updating software, using strong passwords, and being cautious of phishing emails. By following these best practices and staying informed about the latest cybersecurity threats, individuals can protect themselves and their work in an increasingly digital world.

Chapter 8: Programming Language Best Practices

Clean Code Principles

Clean code principles are essential for anyone learning new tech skills, especially in areas such as web development, mobile app development, cybersecurity, programming language, user experience design, and artificial intelligence. Clean code refers to writing code that is easy to read, understand, and maintain. By following clean code principles, developers can improve the quality of their code, reduce bugs, and enhance the overall efficiency of their projects.

One of the key principles of clean code is to write code that is easy to understand. This means using clear and descriptive variable names, avoiding overly complex logic, and breaking down large functions into smaller, more manageable pieces. By writing code that is easy to understand, developers can make their projects more accessible to team members and future collaborators.

Another important principle of clean code is to write code that is easy to test. This involves writing unit tests for individual functions and modules, as well as integration tests to ensure that different parts of the code work together correctly. By writing code that is easy to test, developers can catch bugs early in the development process and ensure that their projects are robust and reliable.

Clean code also emphasizes the importance of writing code that is easy to maintain. This involves following best practices such as using consistent formatting, documenting code thoroughly, and refactoring code regularly to keep it clean and organized. By writing code that is easy to maintain, developers can save time and effort in the long run by making it easier to add new features, fix bugs, and improve performance.

In conclusion, clean code principles are a crucial aspect of learning new tech skills in areas such as web development, mobile app development, cybersecurity, programming language, user experience design, and artificial intelligence. By following these principles, developers can write code that is easy to understand, test, and maintain, leading to higher quality projects and more efficient development processes. It is essential for aspiring tech professionals to prioritize clean code practices in order to succeed in their respective fields.

Code Refactoring Techniques

Code refactoring is a crucial skill for anyone learning new tech skills, particularly in the fields of web development, mobile app development, cybersecurity, programming language, user experience design, and artificial intelligence. Refactoring refers to the process of restructuring existing computer code without changing its external behavior. This practice helps improve the code's readability, maintainability, and overall quality, making it easier to work with in the long run.

One common code refactoring technique is extracting methods. This involves breaking down a long, complex method into smaller, more manageable chunks. By doing so, you can improve readability, reduce duplication, and make the code easier to understand and maintain. This technique is especially useful in web development and mobile app development, where codebases can quickly become large and unwieldy.

Another key refactoring technique is renaming variables and methods. Giving meaningful and descriptive names to variables and methods can greatly enhance the readability and maintainability of your code. This practice is essential in cybersecurity, where clear and concise code is crucial for identifying and fixing security vulnerabilities. By following this technique, you can make your code more self-explanatory and easier to work with in the future.

In the realm of programming languages, the technique of removing duplication is a valuable refactoring strategy. Duplicated code is not only harder to maintain but also increases the risk of introducing bugs. By identifying and eliminating duplicate code, you can make your codebase more efficient, reduce the chances of errors, and improve overall code quality. This technique is particularly important in artificial intelligence, where complex algorithms and data structures require careful attention to detail.

In user experience design, code refactoring plays a vital role in ensuring a seamless and intuitive user interface. By simplifying and organizing the codebase, you can create a more user-friendly experience for your audience. Refactoring techniques such as extracting classes and methods, renaming variables, and removing duplication can help streamline the development process and improve the overall user experience. By mastering these code refactoring techniques, you can enhance your skills in web development, mobile app development, cybersecurity, programming languages, user experience design, and artificial intelligence, setting yourself apart as a proficient and knowledgeable tech professional.

Testing and Debugging Strategies

Testing and debugging are essential components of the software development process, as they help ensure that the code functions correctly and efficiently. In this subchapter, we will explore various strategies that can be employed to test and debug code effectively. By mastering these techniques, individuals learning new tech skills in areas such as web development, mobile app development, cybersecurity, programming language, user experience design, and artificial intelligence can improve the quality of their code and enhance their problem-solving abilities.

One important testing strategy is unit testing, which involves testing individual components or units of code in isolation. By isolating specific functions or modules and testing them independently, developers can quickly identify and fix any errors or bugs that may arise. Unit testing also helps ensure that each component of the code base functions as intended, ultimately leading to a more robust and reliable software application.

Another testing strategy that individuals learning new tech skills should be familiar with is integration testing. Integration testing involves testing the interactions between different components or modules of the code base to ensure that they work together seamlessly. By simulating real-world scenarios and testing how different parts of the code interact with each other, developers can identify and rectify any issues that may arise when integrating multiple components.

In addition to testing, debugging is another crucial aspect of the software development process. Debugging involves identifying and fixing errors, bugs, and issues in the code base to ensure that the software application functions correctly. One effective debugging strategy is using debugging tools and techniques, such as breakpoints, watchpoints, and logging, to identify and isolate bugs in the code. By strategically using these tools, developers can pinpoint the root cause of the problem and implement a solution effectively.

Overall, mastering testing and debugging strategies is essential for individuals learning new tech skills in various niches, including web development, mobile app development, cybersecurity, programming language, user experience design, and artificial intelligence. By incorporating these techniques into their development workflow, developers can improve the quality and reliability of their code, ultimately leading to more successful software applications. With practice and dedication, individuals can become proficient in testing and debugging, ensuring that their code meets the highest standards of quality and performance.

Chapter 9: User Experience Design Principles

Importance of User Experience

In the world of technology, user experience plays a crucial role in the success of any project. Whether you are developing a website, a mobile app, or a cybersecurity tool, the way users interact with your product can make or break its success. This subchapter will explore the importance of user experience and how it can impact various tech skills such as web development, mobile app development, cybersecurity, programming languages, user experience design, and artificial intelligence.

For people learning new tech skills, understanding the importance of user experience is essential for creating successful projects. By focusing on the needs and expectations of users, developers can create products that are intuitive, easy to use, and visually appealing. This can lead to increased user satisfaction, higher engagement, and ultimately, greater success for the project.

In the realm of web development skills, user experience is crucial for creating websites that are user-friendly and accessible. By designing websites with the user in mind, developers can ensure that visitors have a positive experience and are more likely to return. This can lead to higher conversion rates, increased traffic, and improved search engine rankings.

Similarly, in mobile app development skills, user experience is key to creating apps that are engaging and easy to use. By focusing on usability, functionality, and aesthetics, developers can create apps that users will love to use. This can lead to higher app downloads, increased user retention, and better reviews in the app store.

In cybersecurity skills, user experience is important for creating secure and user-friendly tools that protect sensitive data. By designing cybersecurity tools with a focus on usability and accessibility, developers can ensure that users are able to easily navigate and understand the security features of the product. This can lead to better adoption of cybersecurity practices and increased protection against cyber threats.

Design Thinking Process

In the realm of technology, the design thinking process is a crucial framework that guides the creation of innovative solutions to complex problems. Whether you are delving into web development, mobile app development, cybersecurity, programming languages, user experience design, or artificial intelligence, mastering the design thinking process is essential for success in these fields. This subchapter will explore the key principles and steps of the design thinking process, offering valuable insights for people learning new tech skills.

At its core, the design thinking process is a human-centered approach to problem-solving that emphasizes empathy, creativity, and collaboration. It involves a series of iterative steps that encourage designers to deeply understand the needs and desires of end users, brainstorm innovative solutions, and rapidly prototype and test ideas. By embracing this process, tech professionals can cultivate a mindset that values experimentation, failure, and continuous learning.

The first step in the design thinking process is empathize, where designers immerse themselves in the experiences of users to gain insights into their needs, goals, and pain points. This phase involves conducting interviews, surveys, and observations to uncover valuable data that informs the design process. By empathizing with users, tech professionals can develop a deep understanding of the context in which their solutions will be used, leading to more meaningful and impactful outcomes.

The next step in the design thinking process is define, where designers distill their research findings into a clear problem statement that frames the design challenge. This phase involves synthesizing data, identifying patterns, and articulating the core issues that need to be addressed. By defining the problem statement, tech professionals can ensure that their design efforts are focused and purposeful, setting the stage for effective solution development.

Following the define phase is ideate, where designers engage in brainstorming sessions to generate a wide range of creative solutions to the defined problem. This phase involves suspending judgment, encouraging wild ideas, and exploring unconventional approaches to design challenges. By embracing a spirit of curiosity and experimentation, tech professionals can unlock new possibilities and push the boundaries of what is possible in their work.

Usability Testing Methods

Usability testing is a crucial step in the development process of any technology project. It involves evaluating a product or system by testing it with real users to determine its usability, efficiency, and effectiveness. In this subchapter, we will explore various usability testing methods that can be applied to improve the user experience of web and mobile applications, cybersecurity tools, programming languages, user interfaces, and artificial intelligence systems.

One of the most common usability testing methods is the think-aloud protocol, where users are asked to verbalize their thoughts and actions as they interact with the product. This method provides valuable insights into how users perceive and navigate the system, allowing developers to identify potential issues and make necessary improvements. It is particularly useful for understanding user behavior and preferences in real-time.

Another effective usability testing method is the task-based approach, where users are given specific tasks to complete using the product. This method helps developers assess the system's functionality and ease of use, as well as identify any obstacles or inefficiencies that may hinder the user experience. By observing how users interact with the product to accomplish tasks, developers can gather valuable feedback on the interface design and overall usability.

A/B testing is another popular usability testing method that involves comparing two versions of a product to determine which one performs better in terms of usability and user satisfaction. By randomly assigning users to either version A or version B, developers can analyze user behavior and feedback to identify the strengths and weaknesses of each design. This method allows for data-driven decision-making and iterative improvements based on user preferences and performance metrics.

Heuristic evaluation is a usability testing method that involves expert evaluators inspecting the product against a set of established usability principles or heuristics. By applying their knowledge and experience, evaluators can identify potential usability issues and provide recommendations for improvement. This method is particularly useful for identifying usability problems early in the development process and ensuring that the product meets user needs and expectations.

In conclusion, usability testing methods play a critical role in enhancing the user experience of technology projects across various domains, including web development, mobile app development, cybersecurity, programming languages, user interfaces, and artificial intelligence. By incorporating these methods into the development process, developers can gather valuable feedback, identify usability issues, and make informed decisions to create products that are intuitive, efficient, and user-friendly.

Chapter 10: Artificial Intelligence Basics

Introduction to AI

In today's rapidly advancing technological landscape, the field of Artificial Intelligence (AI) plays a crucial role in shaping the future of various industries. From web development to cybersecurity, AI has the potential to revolutionize the way we approach problem-solving and decision-making. In this subchapter, we will delve into the fundamentals of AI and explore how it can be leveraged to enhance your skills in web development, mobile app development, cybersecurity, programming languages, user experience design, and more.

AI refers to the simulation of human intelligence processes by machines, particularly computer systems. It encompasses a wide range of technologies such as machine learning, natural language processing, and computer vision. By understanding the principles behind AI, you can unlock new opportunities to automate tasks, analyze data, and make informed decisions in your projects. Whether you are a beginner or an experienced professional, grasping the basics of AI is essential for staying competitive in today's tech-driven world.

In the realm of web development, AI can be used to enhance user experiences, personalize content, and optimize website performance. By incorporating AI-powered chatbots, recommendation systems, and predictive analytics, developers can create dynamic and engaging websites that cater to the unique needs of their users. Additionally, AI can help streamline the development process by automating repetitive tasks and identifying potential vulnerabilities in the codebase.

For mobile app developers, AI offers a wealth of opportunities to create intelligent and intuitive applications. By integrating AI algorithms into mobile apps, developers can enable features such as voice recognition, image recognition, and predictive text input.

These capabilities not only enhance the user experience but also make apps more efficient and user-friendly. Furthermore, AI can be used to analyze user behavior, gather insights, and improve app performance over time.

In the realm of cybersecurity, AI plays a critical role in detecting and mitigating threats in real-time. By leveraging AI-powered tools, cybersecurity professionals can monitor network activity, identify suspicious patterns, and respond to security incidents with greater speed and accuracy. AI algorithms can also be used to predict emerging threats, analyze vulnerabilities, and strengthen the overall security posture of an organization. By mastering AI skills, cybersecurity professionals can stay ahead of cybercriminals and protect sensitive data effectively.

In conclusion, AI is a transformative technology that has the potential to reshape the way we approach various tech skills. Whether you are a web developer, mobile app developer, cybersecurity expert, programmer, user experience designer, or aspiring AI specialist, understanding the fundamentals of AI is essential for unlocking new opportunities and staying competitive in the digital age. By exploring the principles and applications of AI, you can enhance your skills, tackle complex challenges, and drive innovation in your chosen field.

Machine Learning Algorithms

Machine learning algorithms are an essential component of modern technology and are utilized in a wide range of applications, from web development to artificial intelligence. In this subchapter, we will explore the fundamentals of machine learning algorithms and how they can be applied in various fields. Whether you are learning new tech skills for web development, mobile app development, cybersecurity, programming language, user experience design, or artificial intelligence, understanding machine learning algorithms is crucial for success in today's digital world.

Machine learning algorithms are a set of rules and statistical models that computer systems use to perform specific tasks without being explicitly programmed. These algorithms allow computers to learn from data, make predictions, and improve their performance over time. By analyzing patterns in data, machine learning algorithms can identify trends, detect anomalies, and make decisions based on past experiences. This process is known as training the algorithm, where it learns from labeled data to make accurate predictions on new, unseen data.

There are various types of machine learning algorithms, each suited for different tasks and data types. Supervised learning algorithms, such as linear regression and support vector machines, require labeled data to make predictions. Unsupervised learning algorithms, like clustering and dimensionality reduction, do not rely on labeled data and instead find patterns in unlabeled data. Reinforcement learning algorithms, such as Q-learning and deep Q-networks, use a reward system to learn optimal actions in a given environment. Understanding the differences between these types of algorithms is essential for choosing the right approach for your specific problem.

In the realm of web development, machine learning algorithms can be used to personalize content, improve search results, and detect fraudulent activities. In mobile app development, these algorithms can enhance user experiences, automate tasks, and optimize performance. In cybersecurity, machine learning algorithms play a crucial role in detecting and preventing cyber threats, identifying vulnerabilities, and securing networks. For those interested in programming language skills, understanding machine learning algorithms can open up new opportunities for developing innovative software solutions. In user experience design, these algorithms can help create personalized interfaces, improve usability, and enhance user engagement. And in the field of artificial intelligence, machine learning algorithms are at the core of developing intelligent systems that can learn, reason, and make decisions autonomously.

As you continue to learn new tech skills in web development, mobile app development, cybersecurity, programming language, user experience design, and artificial intelligence, mastering machine learning algorithms will give you a competitive edge in today's fast-paced digital landscape. By understanding the fundamentals of these algorithms and how they can be applied in various fields, you will be better equipped to solve complex problems, innovate new solutions, and advance your career in the tech industry. So, dive into the world of machine learning algorithms and unleash your potential as a tech-savvy professional.

Neural Networks and Deep Learning

Neural networks and deep learning are fundamental concepts in the field of artificial intelligence and programming. These technologies have revolutionized the way we approach problem-solving in various industries, including web development, mobile app development, cybersecurity, programming language development, user experience design, and more. Understanding how neural networks and deep learning work is essential for anyone looking to enhance their skills in these areas.

Neural networks are computational models inspired by the human brain's structure and function. They are composed of interconnected nodes called neurons, which process and transmit information through weighted connections. Deep learning is a subset of neural networks that involves multiple layers of neurons, allowing for complex patterns to be learned and recognized. These technologies have been used to develop powerful algorithms for tasks such as image and speech recognition, natural language processing, and autonomous decision-making.

In the context of web development, neural networks and deep learning can be used to create intelligent systems that personalize user experiences, analyze user behavior, and automate tasks. Mobile app developers can leverage these technologies to enhance app functionality, improve user engagement, and optimize app performance. In cybersecurity, neural networks and deep learning can be utilized to detect and prevent cyber threats, identify anomalies in network traffic, and enhance data security measures.

For programmers, understanding neural networks and deep learning opens up new possibilities for developing advanced algorithms, optimizing code performance, and solving complex problems. User experience designers can use these technologies to create more intuitive and interactive interfaces, improve user engagement, and personalize user experiences. As artificial intelligence continues to evolve, knowledge of neural networks and deep learning will become increasingly valuable in a wide range of industries and applications.

In conclusion, mastering neural networks and deep learning is crucial for anyone looking to advance their skills in web development, mobile app development, cybersecurity, programming languages, user experience design, and artificial intelligence. By understanding the principles behind these technologies and exploring their practical applications, individuals can unlock new opportunities for innovation, problem-solving, and creativity in the ever-evolving tech landscape.

Chapter 11: Putting It All Together

Project-Based Learning Approach

In the world of technology, mastering programming languages is essential for individuals looking to excel in various fields such as web development, mobile app development, cybersecurity, programming language skills, user experience design, and artificial intelligence. One effective approach to learning these languages is through project-based learning. This method allows individuals to apply their theoretical knowledge to real-world projects, enhancing their understanding and skill development.

By engaging in project-based learning, individuals are able to gain hands-on experience in coding, debugging, and problem-solving. This approach not only helps learners understand the syntax and semantics of programming languages but also enables them to see how these languages are used in practical applications. Through working on projects, individuals can develop their creativity, critical thinking, and collaboration skills, which are crucial in the tech industry.

Additionally, project-based learning allows individuals to build a portfolio of projects that showcase their skills and expertise to potential employers. This hands-on experience can give learners a competitive edge in the job market and increase their chances of landing their desired roles in web development, mobile app development, cybersecurity, programming language skills, user experience design, or artificial intelligence.

Moreover, project-based learning encourages individuals to work on projects that align with their interests and career goals. This personalized approach to learning not only keeps learners engaged and motivated but also allows them to explore different aspects of programming languages and technologies. By working on projects that excite them, individuals can deepen their understanding of the languages and enhance their problem-solving abilities.

In conclusion, project-based learning is a highly effective approach for individuals learning new tech skills in web development, mobile app development, cybersecurity, programming language skills, user experience design, and artificial intelligence. This method provides a practical and hands-on way for learners to master programming languages, develop essential skills, build a portfolio, and explore their interests. By embracing project-based learning, individuals can set themselves up for success in the ever-evolving tech industry.

Building Real-World Applications

Building Real-World Applications is an essential step in mastering programming languages such as Python, Java, and C++. For people learning new tech skills in various niches such as web development, mobile app development, cybersecurity, programming language, user experience design, and artificial intelligence, understanding how to apply their knowledge in real-world scenarios is crucial. This subchapter will explore the importance of building real-world applications and provide practical tips on how to do so effectively.

One of the key benefits of building real-world applications is the opportunity to put theoretical knowledge into practice. By working on actual projects, learners can gain a deeper understanding of how programming languages work and how they can be used to solve real-world problems. This hands-on experience is invaluable for anyone looking to build a career in tech, as it allows them to develop the practical skills needed to succeed in the industry.

In addition to gaining practical experience, building real-world applications also allows learners to showcase their skills to potential employers or clients. By creating a portfolio of projects that demonstrate their abilities, individuals can increase their chances of landing job opportunities or securing freelance work. This can be especially beneficial for those looking to break into competitive fields such as web development, mobile app development, and cybersecurity.

When building real-world applications, it is important to choose projects that align with your interests and career goals. By working on projects that are personally meaningful, learners are more likely to stay motivated and engaged throughout the development process. Additionally, focusing on projects that are relevant to your desired niche can help you build a strong portfolio that demonstrates your expertise in that area.

Finally, building real-world applications is a great way to continue learning and improving your skills. As you work on projects, you will inevitably encounter challenges and obstacles that require you to problem-solve and think creatively. By overcoming these challenges, you will not only strengthen your programming skills but also develop valuable problem-solving abilities that are essential for success in the tech industry.

Continuous Learning and Skill Development

Continuous learning and skill development are crucial for individuals seeking to excel in the fast-paced world of technology. Whether you are interested in web development, mobile app development, cybersecurity, programming languages, user experience design, or artificial intelligence, staying up to date with the latest trends and best practices is essential. In this subchapter, we will explore the importance of continuous learning and provide practical tips on how to enhance your skills in the ever-evolving field of technology.

In the rapidly changing landscape of technology, it is imperative for individuals to commit themselves to continuous learning. By staying abreast of the latest developments and advancements in your chosen niche, you can ensure that your skills remain relevant and marketable. This commitment to learning will not only benefit your career but also enhance your problem-solving abilities and critical thinking skills.

One of the best ways to continuously develop your skills in technology is to engage in ongoing education and training. Whether through formal education programs, online courses, workshops, or self-study, there are countless resources available for individuals looking to enhance their skills in areas such as web development, mobile app development, cybersecurity, programming languages, user experience design, and artificial intelligence. By taking advantage of these resources, you can stay ahead of the curve and adapt to the ever-changing demands of the tech industry.

Additionally, networking with other professionals in your field can also be a valuable tool for continuous learning and skill development. By joining industry groups, attending conferences, and participating in online forums, you can gain insights from others, share knowledge, and stay informed about the latest trends and technologies. Collaborating with like-minded individuals can provide you with new perspectives and fresh ideas, helping you to expand your skill set and stay competitive in the field of technology.

In conclusion, continuous learning and skill development are essential for individuals seeking to succeed in the dynamic and rapidly evolving world of technology. By committing to ongoing education, training, and networking, you can enhance your skills in areas such as web development, mobile app development, cybersecurity, programming languages, user experience design, and artificial intelligence. By staying informed, adaptable, and open to new ideas, you can position yourself as a knowledgeable and skilled professional in the ever-changing landscape of technology.

Conclusion: Mastering Programming Languages - Recap of Key Concepts - Tips for Continued Growth in Tech Skills - Resources for Further Learning and Practice

In conclusion, mastering programming languages is a crucial step in advancing your tech skills and career in fields such as web development, mobile app development, cybersecurity, programming language, user experience design, and artificial intelligence. Throughout this book, we have covered key concepts in Python, Java, and C++, three of the most widely used programming languages in the tech industry. By understanding the fundamentals of these languages, you will be better equipped to tackle complex projects and solve real-world problems.

To recap, some of the key concepts we have covered include variables, data types, control structures, functions, classes, and object-oriented programming. These concepts serve as the building blocks for writing efficient and maintainable code in any programming language. By mastering these concepts, you will be able to write code that is not only functional but also elegant and easy to understand for yourself and others.

As you continue to grow your tech skills, it is important to stay updated on the latest trends and advancements in the industry. One tip for continued growth is to actively seek out new learning opportunities, whether through online courses, workshops, or networking events. By staying curious and open to learning new things, you will be better prepared to adapt to the ever-changing tech landscape.

For those looking to further enhance their programming language skills, there are plenty of resources available for learning and practice. Online platforms like Codecademy, Coursera, and Udemy offer a wide range of courses on Python, Java, C++, and other programming languages. Additionally, community forums like Stack Overflow and GitHub provide a wealth of knowledge and support for developers at all levels. By taking advantage of these resources, you can continue to sharpen your skills and stay ahead in the competitive tech industry.

In conclusion, mastering programming languages is a continuous journey that requires dedication, practice, and a willingness to learn. By understanding the key concepts, staying updated on industry trends, and leveraging resources for further learning and practice, you can build a strong foundation in tech skills and advance your career in fields such as web development, mobile app development, cybersecurity, programming language, user experience design, and artificial intelligence. Keep pushing yourself to learn and grow, and you will undoubtedly achieve success in the ever-evolving world of technology.

"Program Language Mastery" is a comprehensive guide for programmers looking to deepen their understanding and proficiency in various programming languages. The book covers a wide range of languages, including Python, Java, C++, and more, providing detailed explanations of key concepts, best practices, and advanced techniques. With practical examples and exercises, readers are able to apply their knowledge and hone their skills in each language. Whether you are a beginner or an experienced programmer, "Program Language Mastery" offers valuable insights and strategies for mastering multiple programming languages.

www.ingramcontent.com/pod-product-compliance
Lightning Source LLC
LaVergne TN
LVHW051622050326
832903LV00033B/4622